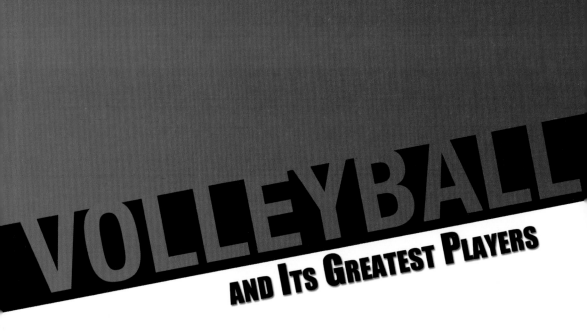

VOLLEYBALL

AND ITS GREATEST PLAYERS

in**side** *sports*

VOLLEYBALL
AND ITS GREATEST PLAYERS

EDITED BY SHALINI SAXENA

Britannica®
Educational Publishing
IN ASSOCIATION WITH

ROSEN
EDUCATIONAL SERVICES

Published in 2015 by Britannica Educational Publishing (a trademark of Encyclopædia Britannica, Inc.) in association with The Rosen Publishing Group, Inc.
29 East 21st Street, New York, NY 10010

Distributed exclusively by Rosen Publishing.
To see additional Britannica Educational Publishing titles, go to rosenpublishing.com.

First Edition

Britannica Educational Publishing
J.E. Luebering: Director, Core Reference Group
Anthony L. Green: Editor, Compton's by Britannica

Rosen Publishing
Hope Lourie Killcoyne: Executive Editor
Shalini Saxena: Editor
Nelson Sá: Art Director
Michael Moy: Designer
Cindy Reiman: Photography Manager
Introduction and supplementary material by Susan Meyer

Library of Congress Cataloging-in-Publication Data

Volleyball and its greatest players/edited by Shalini Saxena.—First Edition.
        pages cm.—((Inside Sports))
"Distributed exclusively by Rosen Publishing"—T.p. verso.
Includes bibliographical references and index.
ISBN 978-1-62275-594-3 (library bound)
1. Volleyball—History—Juvenile literature. 2. Volleyball players—Rating of. I. Saxena, Shalini, 1982–
GV1015.34.V65 2015
796.325—dc23

                                                                      2014023011

Manufactured in the United States of America

On the cover, page 3: Angela Leyva. Cris *Bouroncle/AFP/Getty Images*

Pages 6-7, 10, 21, 33, 41, 70, 71, 73, 76, 78 © iStockphoto.com/Matt Brown; pp. 18, 19, 26, 35, 36 ratch/Shutterstock.com; back cover, interior pages background image Ruggiero S/iStock/Thinkstock; silhouettes Bojanovic/Shutterstock.com;

CONTENTS

INTRODUCTION

In 2004, the Peace and Friendship Stadium in Athens was packed with Olympic fans excited to watch the men's volleyball quarterfinal match between the United States and Greece. It was an eagerly anticipated match not only because it involved the Olympic host country's team, but also because two years earlier at the Fédération Internationale de Volleyball (FIVB) World Championships, Greece had beaten the United States in a thrilling upset. In Athens, after dropping two of the first three sets to Greece, the U.S. team again found itself behind in the fourth set of the match, at one point trailing Greece by a seemingly insurmountable 12–20 margin. If Greece won the set, they would win the match and advance on. In a bold move, the U.S. team coach Doug Beal made the difficult decision to take out star setter and three-time Olympian Lloy Ball and replace him with a younger player, Donald Suxho. The gamble worked and, with

A member of Greece's volleyball team spikes the ball against the U.S. team during the men's quarterfinal match at the 2004 Olympic Games in Athens. The thrilling match ended with a U.S. win. **Al Bello/Getty Images**

Ball encouraging his teammates from the sidelines, the Americans rallied to win the fourth set 25–23. Ball returned to the match as a substitute server in the fifth set, which the U.S. team won 17–15 to complete one of the most dramatic comebacks in Olympic volleyball history.

As that classic match in Athens showed, volleyball is a sport that depends both on the strengths of the individual players and the way players work together as a team. Unlike the majority of team competitive sports, opposing teams in volleyball don't have any physical contact with each other. Instead the two teams of six players are separated by a net. Despite this limited contact, volleyball can be one of the most fast-paced and exciting of team sports. Each team member has a specific skill set and each must work together in perfect communication to receive the ball and return it over the net. They must dive, jump, and run across the court with strength and agility.

Volleyball originated in the United States over one hundred years ago. Since then it has rapidly grown in popularity around the world. According to sports blog *Sporteology*, volleyball is the sixth most popular sport in the world with around 800 million participants globally. In the United States, the sport has also achieved popularity, particularly at the high school and college levels. In indoor volleyball, a large percentage of the participants are female. In fact, according to a 2013 National High School Athletics Survey, for every high school boy playing volleyball, there are eight more girls. In the sport of beach volleyball, the gender divide is less.

This book will explore some of the basic rules and strategies of the game of volleyball. It will provide a history of how the game was first invented and its exciting evolution into a globally played sport and a major event at the Summer Olympics. It will also look at the different skills that all volleyball players must master and the different positions players may specialize in on the court. It will explore some of the differences between the sports of indoor volleyball and beach volleyball and look at some of the truly great players in each sport. While there are masters of volleyball around the world, the focus of this book will be primarily on those from the United States.

From beach volleyball to the indoor court, volleyball has brought thrilling victories and stunning upsets, masterful athletes, and feats of athleticism. For hundreds of millions of fans around the world, it is an exciting game to watch and even more fun to play.

CHAPTER 1
RULES OF THE GAME

Volleyball is a team sport in which players use their hands or arms to knock a ball over a net. Two teams, usually with six players each, compete in a volleyball game. Volleyball requires a minimum of equipment and space and can be played indoors or outdoors.

COURT AND EQUIPMENT

The indoor game is played on a smooth-surfaced court 9 meters (30 feet) wide by 18 meters (60 feet) long, divided by a center line into two equal areas, one of which is selected by or assigned to each of the two competing teams. Players may not step completely beyond the center line while the ball is in play. A line 3 meters (10 feet) from and parallel to the center line of each half of the court indicates the point in front of which a back court player may not

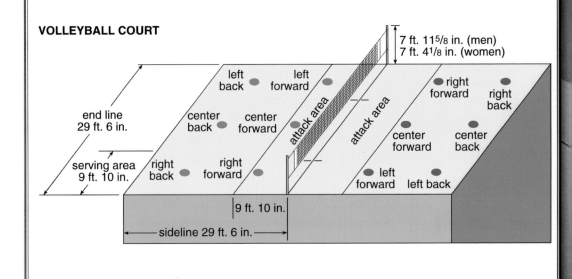

VOLLEYBALL COURT

7 ft. 11 5/8 in. (men)
7 ft. 4 1/8 in. (women)

left back   left forward   right forward   right back

end line 29 ft. 6 in.

center back   center forward   center forward   center back

attack area   attack area

serving area 9 ft. 10 in.

right back   right forward   left forward   left back

9 ft. 10 in.

sideline 29 ft. 6 in.

An indoor volleyball court consists of two adjacent squares, each measuring 29 feet 6 inches on a side and separated by a net. Players advance position with each change of serve. The player at the right back position serves. **Encyclopædia Britannica, Inc.**

drive the ball over the net from a position above the top of the net. (This offensive action, called a spike, or kill, is usually performed most effectively and with greatest power near the net by the forward line of players.) A tightly stretched net is placed across the court exactly above the middle of the center line; official net heights (measured from the top edge of the net to the playing surface—in the middle of the court) are 2.4 meters (8 feet) for men and 2.2 meters

(7.4 feet) for women. Further adjustments in net height can be made for young people and others who need a lower net. A vertical tape marker is attached to the net directly above each side boundary line of the court, and, to help game officials judge whether served or volleyed balls are in or out of bounds, a flexible antenna extends 1 meter (3 feet) above the net along the outer edge of each vertical tape marker. The ball used is around 260 to 280 grams (9 to 10 ounces) and is inflated to about 65 cm (25.6 inches) in circumference.

A ball must pass over the net entirely between the antennae. A service area, traditionally 3 meters (10 feet) long, is marked outside and behind the right one-third of each court end line. At the 1996 Olympic Games, the service area was extended to 9 meters (30 feet). The service must be made from within or behind this area. A space at least 2 meters (6 feet) wide around the entire court is needed to permit freedom of action, eliminate hazards from obstructions, and allow space for net support posts and the officials' stands. A clear area above the court at least 8 meters (26 feet) high is required to permit the ball to be served or received and played without interference.

Beach volleyball is usually played, as its name implies, on a sand court with two players per team. The court dimensions for beach volleyball are 8 meters (26 feet) by 16 meters (52 feet), making it slightly smaller than the court space used in indoor volleyball. Also, unlike on the indoor volleyball court, in beach volleyball the court has no attack line designated 3 meters

A beach volleyball court has many of the features found on an indoor court. However, a beach court is smaller and has no attack line near the net. **Matej Divizna/Getty Images**

(10 feet) from the net. The net height in beach volleyball remains the same as on the indoor court.

PLAYING THE GAME

Informally, any number can play volleyball. In competition, each team consists of six players, three of whom take the forward positions in a row close to and facing the net, the other three playing the back court. (An exception to this rotation is the *libero*, a position introduced at the 2000 Olympics.) Serves are made underhand or overhand with an open hand or fist.

Play is started when the right back (the person on the right of the second row) of the serving team steps outside his end line into the serving area and bats the ball with a hand, fist, or arm over the net into the opponents' half of the court. The opponents receive the ball and return it across the net in a series of not more than three contacts with the ball. This must be done without any player catching or holding the ball while it is in play and without

During a game, a team usually has six players on the court: three in the front and three in the rear. Ververidis Vasilis/Shutterstock.com

any player touching the net or entering the opponents' court area. The ball must not touch the floor, and a player may not

Volleyball games always begin with a ball being served over the net. Serves can be made underhand, as seen here, or overhead. **Walter Lockwood/Photodisc/Getty Images**

touch the ball twice in succession. A player continues to serve until his team makes an error, commits a foul, or completes the game. When the service changes, the receiving team becomes the serving team and its players rotate clockwise one position, the right forward shifting to the right back position and then serving from the service area. Either team can score, with points being awarded for successfully hitting the ball onto the opposing side's half of the court, as well as when the opposing side commits errors or fouls, such as hitting the ball out of bounds, failing to return the ball, contacting the ball more than three times before returning it, etc. Only one point at a time is scored for a successful play. A game is won by the team that first scores 25 points, provided the winning team is ahead by 2 or more points, except in the fifth set, when a team needs to score only 15 points and win by 2 points.

By the time the 2000 Olympics were held, several rule changes to international competition had taken effect. One change created the *libero*, a player on each team who serves as a defensive specialist. The *libero* wears a different color from the rest of the team and is not allowed to serve or rotate to the front line.

RULE CHANGES

In 1998, two significant rule changes were instituted by volleyball's international organization—the Fédération Internationale de Volleyball (FIVB)—to speed up the sport, which often included matches on the elite level that lasted more than three hours. The creation of the *libero* position added more defense

The libero *position was introduced at the Olympic Games for the first time in 2000, becoming an important feature of matches such as this one between the U.S. and Russian women's volleyball teams.* Darren McNamara/Getty Images

and specialization to the sport. The *libero* was a defensive specialist who was allowed an unlimited number of substitutions to play in the back row. The *libero* could not serve, block, or set the ball in front of the 3-meter (10 foot) line. This new rule, which began as an experiment in 1996 and was used at each of the major international events in 1998, allowed smaller volleyball players to play on the international level. The experiment was fully adopted for the 1999 campaign, and *liberos* appeared on teams at the 2000 Olympics.

The FIVB also changed to the scoring system for international volleyball matches. The scoring system for the best-three-of-five matches was altered so that the first team to register 25 points in rally scoring (and to lead by two points) would win the game. This rule was installed for the first four games of each match, while the fifth game is played to 15 points. Teams are allowed to score regardless of whether they served or started on defense. Previously, rally scoring was used in the fifth games, and only the serving team could score points during the first four games.

Another important rule change allowed the defensive side to score, whereas formerly only the serving team was awarded points.

Beach volleyball has a similar gameplay to its indoor counterpart. However, in addition to the obvious differences in the courts and number of players, there are also some key variations in rules. In beach volleyball, teams play the best out of three sets, the first two sets played to 21 points. As in indoor volleyball, the deciding set is played to 15 points. Players are also allowed to hit the ball up to three times while attempting to return it. In beach volleyball, there is no *libero*. Also, in indoor volleyball the opposing teams alternate sides of the court between sets. In beach volleyball, the teams switch sides every 7 points (or every 5 points in the final set).

CHAPTER 2
GAME MECHANICS AND STRATEGY

Volleyball is a game that requires strength, speed, and physical agility. A good player must be able to communicate fluidly with his or her teammates while making split-second decisions. There are six basic skills in volleyball that players must master: passing, setting, spiking, blocking, digging, and serving. Different players will be better equipped for certain skills than others. A good team strategizes using each of its players' strengths and weaknesses in the most effective way.

In order for a volleyball team to be successful, players must be able to coordinate their offensive and defensive skills effectively and communicate clearly. **Michelangelo Gratton/Digital Vision/Getty Images**

POSITIONS

In indoor volleyball, there are six players on each side, including three in the front court and three in the back court. In beach volleyball, there are only two players per side. Players rotate clockwise when their team gains the serve. While different teams have different strategies, often the players on the front row focus on hitting and blocking, while the players behind them are diggers, setters, and passers. Different players usually specialize in different positions depending on their strengths.

BLOCKERS

The middle blocker is the position in the center of an indoor court right in front of the net. The job of the blocker is to stop the ball as it is coming across the net from the opponent's side. The blocker is the key to a team's defense. Blockers can also work on the offensive by throwing the other team's defense off balance. Successful blockers are often tall. Their height gives them an

Three players from the Brigham Young University men's volleyball team jump to block the ball during a game against the University of California, Irvine. Christopher Halloran/Shutterstock.com

advantage at blocking balls closer to the net. A good blocker also needs to be fast—he or she has to get across the court very quickly.

HITTERS

Hitters are an important part of the team's offense and the most likely players to score a point. The outside hitter is the player in the front left side of the court. The outside hitter and the right side hitter receive balls from the setter and knock them over the net. If the hitter drives the ball quickly enough and strategically enough against the opposing side, the opposing team should not be able to return it.

LIBEROS

The *libero* is one of the more unique positions on the court. This player wears a different jersey than the rest of his or her team. *Liberos* only play on the back row, but they can sub in and out for other players there. There is one *libero* on a team, and he or she is the foundation of a team's defense. The *libero* may return the serve. *Liberos* must be skilled at passing and digging. The job of the *libero* is to keep the ball in the air long enough to provide the team with chances to score points.

SETTERS

While many players on the team are focused on defense, the setter is the foundation of a team's offense. The setter decides which player gets the ball and when. The setter usually has the second contact on the ball (after another player has received the serve). He or she delivers the ball to a hitter, who then returns it over the net. The setter has to make split-second decisions and carefully deliver the ball to the hitter.

OPPOSITES

The opposite is so named because in the rotation on court, this player is placed opposite from the setter. The opposite plays on the right side of the court in the front or back. Opposites need to have great blocking skills as well as great hitting skills. This is one position that plays both offense and defense. The opposite is needed to block many shots at the net but

FORMATIONS

In indoor volleyball, there are always six play-ers on the court for each team; however, the formation of these six players can vary. There are three main formations in competitive volleyball. They are described by the num-ber of hitters versus the number of setters, respectively.

4-2 In this formation there are four hitters and two setters. The setters usually set from the middle front or right front positions. The two other front positions are taken by attackers.

6-2 This formation contains six hitters, two of whom also operate as setters. In other words, all players on the court operate as hitters at some point. The three front positions are all attackers, and setters must come forward from the back row to set.

5-1 This formation has five hitters and only one setter. Depending on where the setter is in the rotation, the team may have two hitters or three hitters on the front row.

also contributes to the team as a hitter scoring points. The opposite can take pressure off both the setter and the middle blocker. Different plays and strategies can require different skills from the opposite at any given time.

SKILLS NEEDED

Once the ball is put into play by a serve, the basic object for each team is to keep the ball off the ground when it is on their side and prevent the opposing team from doing the same. Through defensive moves like blocks and digs, and offensive attacks like the spike, players must work in constant teamwork and communication to volley the ball and score points.

BLOCKING

A block is an important defensive move in volleyball. This move is used to stop the ball coming over the net from the opponent's side. An effective block can either return the ball to the opponent's side of the net or slow it down enough so that a teammate can dig the ball. The basic action of a block requires the player to stand facing the net with his or her hands extended overhead. This position allows a player to jump up and make contact with the ball when it comes over the net.

DIGGING

Another important defensive move is the dig. Like a block, a dig is used to prevent the ball from hitting the floor. The difference is that a successful dig usually ends in passing the ball to a teammate who can then return the ball to the opponent's side of the net. To dig

Once a player digs a ball to keep it from hitting the ground, a teammate can take control of the ball in an attempt to return it to the other team. **Christopher Halloran/Shutterstock.com**

a ball, the player maintains a lower stance and uses his or her forearms to make contact with the ball. The player needs to be closer to the ground and ready to stop a ball that is most often coming in a sharp, downward trajectory.

PASSING

In a team sport like volleyball, one of the most important skills to master is executing a good pass. Since each team is allowed to make contact with the ball three times in an

The player on the right makes an overhead pass to a teammate during a match. Passing is essential to ensure that the ball gets to the player best equipped to hit the ball back over the net. **Kirill Kudryavtsev/ AFP/Getty Images**

effort to get it over the net, this means players can also pass the ball two times. Teammates can use these passes to direct the ball to the hitters on the team who can spike the ball into the opponent's court. The key to a good pass is ball control: using the right speed and strength to deliver the ball to a teammate so that he or she can easily receive it.

SERVING

The serve is the move that puts the ball in play. There are two types of serves: underhand and overhand. In an underhand serve, the ball is held in the palm of one hand while the other hand—the hitting hand—is made into a fist. The arm is swung back and the fist makes contact with the ball, knocking it up and over the net. In an overhand serve, the ball is tossed up with one hand while the hitting hand is kept in an open palm. While the ball is still in the air, the hitting hand makes contact, shooting it over the net.

SETTING

A set is a transitional move. The setter receives the pass from a teammate and then passes it to an attacker who can spike the ball over the net. The object of a successful set is to get the ball aloft and provide a well-placed target for the attacker. To do this, the setter receives the ball with his or her hands extended overhead; the ball should make only light contact with the fingertips of the player. It is then set aloft in a controlled movement.

SPIKING

A spike is a powerful attacking movement. It is used to score points on the opposing team by knocking the ball very quickly onto the opposing court and making it difficult for them to return it. A successful spike requires good timing, careful

The spike is an offensive move that can allow a team to score points quickly. When executed correctly, a spike will put the ball on the opposing court without giving the opposing team's defense enough time to respond. wdeon/ Shutterstock.com

observation, and strong follow-through. The attacking player must watch the setter carefully and position himself or herself accordingly. The player then jumps with an arm extended overhead. The hand makes contact with the ball, hitting it down across the net on the opponent's side. For best results, the hand should be slightly in front of the body, and not directly overhead, when it makes contact.

CHAPTER 3

HISTORY OF THE GAME

Volleyball was invented in 1895 by William G. Morgan, physical director of the Young Men's Christian Association (YMCA) in Holyoke, Massachusetts. It was designed as an indoor sport for business-men who found the new game of basketball too vigorous. Morgan called the sport "mintonette," until a professor from Springfield College in Massachusetts noted the volleying nature of play and proposed the name of "volleyball." The origi-nal rules were written by Morgan and printed in the

William G. Morgan. **Courtesy of Springfield College, Babson Library, Archives and Special Collections**

first edition of the *Official Handbook of the Athletic League of the Young Men's Christian Associations of North America* (1897). The game soon proved to have wide appeal for both sexes in schools, playgrounds, the armed forces, and other organizations in the United States, and it was subsequently introduced to other countries.

In 1916, rules were issued jointly by the YMCA and the National Collegiate Athletic Association (NCAA). The first nationwide tournament in the United States was conducted by the National YMCA Physical Education Committee in New York City in 1922. The United States Volleyball Association (USVBA) was formed in 1928 and recognized as the rules-making, governing body in the United States. From 1928 the USVBA—now known as USA Volleyball (USAV)—has conducted annual national men's and senior men's (age 35 and older) volleyball championships, except during 1944 and 1945. Its women's division was started in 1949, and a senior women's division (age 30 and older) was added in 1977. Other national events in the United States are conducted by member groups of the USAV, such as the YMCA and the NCAA.

HOOVERBALL

Hooverball was a medicine-ball game invented in 1929 by Adm. Joel T. Boone, physician to U.S. Pres. Herbert Hoover, in order to keep Hoover physically fit. The sport was nameless until 1931, when a reporter from the *New York Times* christened it "Hooverball" in an article he wrote about the president's daily life.

Hooverball is similar to volleyball and tennis but originated from a popular game called bull-in-the-ring, played by sailors while on board

(continued on the next page)

President Hoover used the medicine balls seen here when he played Hooverball. Although the game is less complex than volleyball or tennis, it requires players to have strength and endurance to handle the weight of the ball. **Library of Congress Prints and Photographs Division Washington**

(continued from the previous page)

ships, in which a sailor in the middle of a circle (the "bull in the ring") tried to intercept a 9-pound (4-kg) medicine ball thrown between the sailors forming the circle. President-elect Hoover witnessed the game played on the battleship *Utah* while returning from a goodwill mission to South America in 1928. After Hoover assumed office, he and Boone decided to adapt that naval game to suit the White House environs and the president's daily routine. Four days after Hoover's inauguration, Hooverball was born.

The game is typically played on a court measuring 20 by 9 meters (66 by 30 feet). A 2.7-kg (6-pound) medicine ball and a 2.4-meter (8-foot) volleyball net are used in the game, which is scored just like tennis. Teams consist of two to four players. The ball is served from the back line, thrown over the net, and, in order to prevent the serving team from scoring a point, the other team must catch the ball on the fly and immediately return it from the point at which the ball was caught. Points are also scored if a team fails to serve or return the ball inbounds.

In the early 21st century, Hooverball experienced modest growth as variations of the game began to be implemented in certain of the unorthodox exercise regimes (such as CrossFit) that became popular at that time. The Herbert Hoover Presidential Library Association in West Branch, Iowa, hosts a Hooverball national championship tournament each year.

INTERNATIONAL INTEREST

Volleyball was introduced into Europe by American troops during World War I, when national organizations were formed. The Fédération Internationale de Volleyball (FIVB) was organized in Paris in 1947 and moved to Lausanne, Switzerland, in 1984. The USVBA was one of the 13 charter members of the FIVB, whose membership grew to 220 member countries by the early 21st century.

International volleyball competition began in 1913 with the first Far East Games, in Manila. During the early 1900s and continuing until after World War II, volleyball in Asia was played on a larger court, with a lower net, and nine players on a team.

The FIVB-sponsored world volleyball championships (for men only in 1949; for both men and women in 1952 and succeeding years) led to acceptance of standardized playing rules and officiating. Volleyball became an Olympic sport for both men and women at the 1964 Olympic Games in Tokyo.

Japan defeated the Soviet Union to win the gold medal in women's volleyball at the Olympic Games of 1964, the first year volleyball was an Olympic sport. **Sankei Archive/ Getty Images**

COMPETITIONS AROUND THE WORLD

European championships were long dominated by Czechoslovakian, Hungarian, Polish, Bulgarian, Romanian, and Soviet (later, Russian) teams. At the world and Olympic level, Soviet teams have won more titles, both men's and women's, than those of any other nation. Their success was attributed to widespread grassroots interest and well-organized play and instruction at all levels of skill. A highly publicized Japanese women's team, Olympic champions in 1964, reflected the interest of private industry in sport. Young women working for the sponsoring company devoted their free time to conditioning, team practice, and competition under expert and demanding coaching. Encouraged by the Japanese Volleyball Association, this women's team made its mark in international competition, winning the World Championship in 1962, 1966, and 1967, in addition to the 1964 Olympics. At the end of the 20th century, however, the Cuban women's team dominated both the World Championships and the Olympics.

The Pan American Games (involving South, Central, and North America) added volleyball in 1955, and Brazil, Mexico, Canada, Cuba, and

The top three teams in men's beach volleyball accept medals at the 2007 Pan American Games. The popularity of volleyball around the world has inspired several international competitions. **Jeff Gross/Getty Images**

the United States are frequent contenders for top honors. In Asia, China, Japan, and Korea dominate competition. Volleyball, especially beach volleyball, is played in Australia, New Zealand, and throughout the South Pacific.

A four-year cycle of international volleyball events, recommended by the FIVB, began in 1969 with World Cup championships, to be held in the year following the Olympic Games; the second year is the World Championships; in the third the regional events are held (e.g.,

Although beach volleyball gained international popularity quickly after its introduction in 1930, it would be more than 50 years before FIVB introduced world championships in the sport and more than 60 years before it was part of the Olympic Games. **Keystone-France/Gamma-Keystone/Getty Images**

European championships, Asian Games, African Games, Pan American Games); and in the fourth year the Olympic Games.

Beach volleyball was introduced in California in 1930. The first official beach volleyball tournament was held in 1948 at Will Rogers State Beach, in Santa Monica, California, and the first FIVB-sanctioned world championship was held in 1986 at Rio de Janeiro. Beach volleyball was added to the roster of the 1996 Olympic Games in Atlanta, Georgia.

CHAPTER 4
NOTABLE PLAYERS

Throughout history there have been a number of men and women who have truly excelled at the game of volleyball. This chapter examines some of these champions of the sport, both in indoor and beach volleyball. The players included only represent the best athletes from the United States; however, there are many around the world who have also made great achievements in the history of volleyball. Some of the players are known for being powerful outsider hitters and others as skilled blockers. Many have achieved medals from various levels of volleyball competition, and several have received multiple gold medals at the Olympic Games while representing Team USA.

LLOY BALL

Lloy Ball is a talented volleyball player who played on the U.S. Olympic men's team four separate times, in 1996, 2000, 2004, and 2008. The team won gold in the 2008 Games in Beijing. Ball was born on February 17,

Lloy Ball holds up his gold medal after the 2008 Olympic Games in Beijing, China. The United States defeated Brazil for the win. **Jonathan Ferrey/Getty Images**

1972, in Fort Wayne, Indiana. His father is Arnie Ball, a well-respected volleyball coach for Indiana University-Purdue University at Fort Wayne, where Lloy attended college. Lloy began playing volleyball when he was just five years old. In 1994, he joined Team USA and within three weeks became its starting setter. For fourteen years, he maintained the position as starting setter. He also served as the captain of Team USA for ten of those years. During his career, Ball has won a bronze medal in the 1994 World Championships, the honor of best server in the world in 1995, best setter in the world in 1999 and 2007, and was captain and starting setter of the 2000 Sydney and 2004 Athens U.S. Olympic teams.

RITA CROCKETT

A member of the Volleyball Hall of Fame and a two-time Olympian, Rita Crockett is one of the finest all-around players in the history of volleyball. Crockett was born on November 2, 1957, in San Antonio, Texas. She was a member of the 1980 U.S. Olympic women's volleyball team. However, because of a U.S. boycott of the games that year, the team did not compete. In 1984, she was again part of the U.S. team, this time leading it to a silver medal. It was the first medal the U.S. women's volleyball team had ever received. Crockett was described by *Sports Illustrated* as "The Rocket" because of her strong vertical leap and powerful shots.

TARA CROSS-BATTLE

Tara Cross-Battle is one of a select few American players to compete at four Olympic Games in indoor volleyball. She was born on September 16, 1968, in Houston, Texas. She played in the position of outside hitter and was known for her skills as an excellent passer and top-notch hitter. She helped provide a strong offense for her team. She joined the U.S. team in 1990 after a strong volleyball career in high school and college. Cross-Battle played with the U.S. team in the Olympics in 1992 (helping it win a bronze medal), in 1996 (when she served as the team captain), 2000, and 2004. Also during her illustrious career, she won gold medals at the World Grand Cup and Canada Cup in 1995. Now retired from professional volleyball, Cross-Battle coaches for the Houston Juniors Volleyball Club.

PHIL DALHAUSSER

As a professional beach volleyball player, Phil Dalhausser has been one half of two very impressive partnerships. He and his former teammate, Todd Rogers, won both the FIVB World Championships in 2007 and the 2008 Olympics in Beijing, representing the United States. Dalhausser was born on January 26, 1980, in Switzerland. He now calls Ventura, California, his hometown. At 6 feet, 9 inches tall, Dalhausser has a long reach, and his height and build have earned him the nickname "The Thin Beast." He played volleyball in college and later teamed up with the player Nick Lucena. However, it was after forming a partnership with Todd Rogers in 2006 that Dalhausser has seen his greatest success. Rogers is a veteran of professional beach volleyball and served as a teammate, mentor, and coach to the younger Dalhausser. From 2008 to 2010, Dalhausser and Rogers won nine out of the thirteen FIVB Grand Slams they played. In 2012, the Dalhausser-Rogers partnership ended, and Dalhausser chose a new partner, Sean Rosenthal, with whom he has scored several more wins, including a gold medal in the 2014 AVP Manhattan Beach Open.

FLO HYMAN

Flora Jean Hyman, known as Flo, was one of the greatest volleyball players of her time. She was born on July 31, 1954, in Inglewood, California. Growing up, Hyman was self-conscious about her height (she would grow to be 6 feet, 5 inches tall). However, she soon found her height helped her in the sports of volleyball and basketball. She was discovered by a coach for the University of Houston while playing beach volleyball. She ended up going to the university on a scholarship. Hyman joined the U.S. national team in 1974. The team qualified for the Moscow Olympics in 1980, but the United States boycotted the Games. Hyman played in the 1984 Olympics and won a silver medal— the first Olympic medal the U.S. women's volleyball team had ever won. Hyman moved to Japan and played professionally on a team called Daiei. She brought the team great success, but planned to move back to the United States for the 1986 season. Unfortunately, she was not given the chance. On January 24, 1986, she collapsed while watching a game courtside and died from a rare heart condition. Despite having her life cut short, she will forever be remembered for her powerful plays and strong leadership.

Flo Hyman prepares to spike the ball during an exhibition game. **Lyn Alweis/Denver Post/Getty Images**

CHARLES "KARCH" KIRALY

Charles "Karch" Kiraly was the first volley-ball player to win three Olympic gold medals and was considered one of the sport's great-est players, excelling at both indoor and beach volleyball.

Kiraly was born on November 3, 1960, in Jackson, Michigan. When Kiraly was four years old, he moved with his family to Santa Barbara, California. His father, Laszlo Kiraly, had played on the Hungarian national volley-ball team, and he introduced his son to the game at an early age; by the time Karch was 11 years old, he had entered his first beach tour-nament with his father. With a vertical leap of 104 centimeters (41 inches), Kiraly was a standout at Santa Barbara High School and during his senior year was named the best player in the state. He attended the University of California (B.S., 1983) in Los Angeles, where he was a four-time All-American and led his squad to three national titles (1979, 1980, 1981) in four years. In 1981 he joined the U.S. national volleyball team, and, as the squad's outside hit-ter, he helped the United States win Olympic gold medals at the 1984 Games in Los Angeles and at the 1988 Games in Seoul, South Korea;

at the latter event he was named the tournament's Most Valuable Player (MVP). The U.S. team also won gold at the 1982 and 1986 World Championships and at the 1987 Pan American Games. In 1986 and 1988, FIVB named Kiraly the best player in the world.

In 1989, Kiraly left the U.S. national team to play with Il Messaggero of Ravenna, Italy, where he was named MVP when the team won the world club championship in 1991. He then concentrated on the financially lucrative beach game that earned him the Association of Volleyball Professionals' MVP title six times (1990, 1992–95, and 1998). At the 1996 Olympic Games in Atlanta, Georgia, beach volleyball debuted as a medal sport, and Kiraly, with partner Kent Steffes, won the gold medal. In 1999, Kiraly surpassed Sinjin Smith as the beach volleyball player with the most victories; by the time of his retirement in 2007, he had won 144 events. He was inducted into the Volleyball Hall of Fame in 2001 and the U.S. Olympic Hall of Fame in 2008. Kiraly wrote several books on volleyball, and his autobiography, *The Sand Man* (written with Byron Shewman), was published in 1999. In 2012, Kiraly was named head coach of the U.S. women's national volleyball team.

Charles "Karch" Kiraly digs a ball during the 2005 AVP Hermosa Beach Open. **Kirby Lee/Getty Images**

MISTY MAY-TREANOR

American beach volleyball player Misty May-Treanor was at the top of her sport in the early 21st century. With her teammate, Kerri Walsh, she won Olympic gold medals in the event in 2004, 2008, and 2012.

Misty May was born on July 30, 1977, in Los Angeles, California. She played indoor volleyball at California State University, Long Beach, where she led her team to the 1998 NCAA title in her senior year. After playing for the U.S. national indoor team at the Pan Am Games, she decided to try her hand at beach volleyball. She teamed with Holly McPeak at the 2000 Olympic Games in Sydney, Australia, finishing fifth after losing in the quarterfinals.

In 2001, May formed her beach volleyball partnership with Walsh, and by the following year they were the number one–ranked team in the world. In 2003, they won a then-record 90 straight matches and all eight tournaments in which they played, including the world championships. That success carried over to the 2004 Olympics in Athens, Greece, in which they became the first American female tandem to win gold in beach volleyball. Following the Athens Games, they captured two more world titles, in 2005 and 2007. Meanwhile, in November 2004, May wed Major League Baseball player Matt Treanor.

At the 2008 Olympics in Beijing, China, May-Treanor and Walsh became the first beach volleyball team to win back-to-back Olympic gold medals. In the final match they ignored a steady downpour and drenched bathing suits to beat Wang Jie and Tian Jia of China 21–18, 21–18. The match was the pair's 108th consecutive victory and their 14th straight Olympics win (they

Misty May-Treanor, left, and her partner, Kerri Walsh, pose after a win against China at the 2007 FIVB Beach Volleyball World Championship in Switzerland. © **AP Images**

did not lose a set either in Beijing or in Athens at the 2004 Olympics).

In their first tournament following the Beijing Games, May-Treanor and Walsh extended their winning streak to 112 matches, but it came to an end on August 31, 2008, with a 21–19, 10–21, 25–23 loss to Olympic teammates Elaine Youngs and Nicole Branagh. The defeat also ended May-Treanor and Walsh's streak of 19 straight tournament titles. Later that year May-Treanor appeared as a contestant on the television show *Dancing with the Stars*. An injury she incurred while rehearsing for the show, however, required surgery on her Achilles tendon, and she missed most of the 2009 season.

In 2011, May-Treanor and Walsh once again competed at the world championships, this time taking home the silver medal. At the Olympic Games in London, England, the following year, the duo won a third consecutive gold medal, defeating fellow Americans April Ross and Jennifer Kessy 21–16, 21–16 in the final. May-Treanor and Walsh did not lose a match in London (although they dropped one set during the preliminary round) and extended their Olympic winning streak to 21 straight matches. May-Treanor retired from competitive play after the London Olympics.

HOLLY McPEAK

Holly McPeak is near the top of many lists. She is a three-time Olympian, has the second highest earnings of any women's professional beach volleyball player ($1.4 million), and the third highest number of career wins (72). McPeak was born on May 15, 1969, in Manhattan Beach, California. She played volleyball through high school and college; at UCLA she led her team to a national championship in 1990. With partner Nancy Reno, McPeak represented the United States at the 1996 Olympic Games in Atlanta, Georgia, but the pair failed to win a medal. McPeak teamed with Misty May-Treanor at the 2000 Olympic Games in Sydney, Australia, but again came away from the Games without a medal after placing fifth. On her third Olympic visit, at the 2004 Athens Games, McPeak, this time playing with Elaine Youngs, earned the United States a bronze medal. McPeak retired in 2009, the same year she was inducted into the Volleyball Hall of Fame. Since retiring from competitive play, McPeak has worked as a commentator and game analyst for the Pac-12 Network.

TODD ROGERS

Todd Rogers is an extremely talented beach volleyball player, best known for his very successful partnership with player Phil Dalhausser. The pair were the champions of the Association of Volleyball Professionals (AVP) Tour from 2007–2008. They also won gold in the 2008 Olympics. Rogers was born on September 20, 1973, in Santa Barbara, California. Growing up and in college, Rogers focused on indoor volleyball. He was named an All-American in 1995 and 1996 for his skills on the court. In 1995, while still a student at the University of California, Santa Barbara, he played in his

Todd Rogers, left, and his partner, Phil Dalhausser, prepare for an incoming ball during a preliminary match at the 2008 Beijing Olympic Games. **Thomas Coex/AFP/Getty Images**

first AVP beach volleyball tournament. From 1996–2001, Rogers played beach volleyball with partner Dax Holdren, with some success. From 2002–2005, he played with Sean Scott. However, it was in 2006, when he began playing with Dalhausser, that the two became a formidable force. They were however defeated at the 2012 Olympics. In 2013, Rogers played the FIVB world tour with a new partner, Ryan Doherty. Rogers changed partners again, teaming up with Theodore Brunner in 2014.

DANIELLE SCOTT-ARRUDA

Danielle Scott-Arruda is an indoor volleyball player in the position of middle blocker who holds the record for most Olympic appearances by any American women's volleyball player. She represented the United States at the Olympics five times consecutively from 1996 to 2012. Scott-Arruda was born on October 1, 1972, in Baton Rouge, Louisiana. She played volleyball throughout her schooling and went to college at California State University, Long Beach State. She led her team to victory in the NCAA National Championships in 1993. Shortly thereafter, she joined the U.S. Olympic team for her first of many appearances on the international stage. She has a number of medals including: four golds and two bronzes from the FIVB World Grand Prix, two silvers from the Olympics (2008 and 2012), and a silver and two bronzes from the FIVB World Cup. She was also named "Best Blocker" at the 2001 FIVB World Grand Prix, 2002 World Championship, and 2009 Pan American Cup.

SINJIN SMITH

Sinjin Smith was a talented beach volleyball player in his own right, but also one half of a powerful duo with his partner, Randy Stoklos. Throughout the late 1980s and early 1990s the pair were considered the "kings of the beach." They tied for the most wins in a single season with 16 wins in 1987. Smith was born on May 7, 1957, in Santa Monica, California. His real name is Christopher St. John Smith, but he started using "Sinjin," which is the Old English pronunciation of St. John. He began to compete in professional beach volleyball tournaments in Southern California when he was only 15. In the late 1970s, Smith played beach volleyball at UCLA. After college, he continued to play, partnering with a former UCLA teammate, Karch Kiraly. After their partnership ended,

Sinjin Smith dives to get the ball during a preliminary match at the 1996 Olympic Games in Atlanta. Joel Robine/AFP/Getty Images

Smith teamed up with Randy Stoklos and the pair began to dominate. Smith has the honor of being the first man to reach 100 career open tournament wins in beach volleyball. Smith retired from competitive volleyball in 2001.

RANDY STOKLOS

A stellar figure in the world of beach volleyball, Randy Stoklos has the honor of being the first player in his sport to earn $1 million in career prize money. With partner Sinjin Smith, Stoklos formed a beach volleyball juggernaut that dominated the competition from the late 1980s to the early 1990s. The pair won the FIVB Beach Volleyball World Tour every year from 1989 to 1992. Stoklos was born December 13, 1960, and grew up in Pacific Palisades, California. He began playing beach volleyball at Muscle Beach in California in 1974, and by 1981, he had won his first Manhattan Beach Open title (with partner Jim Menges); Stoklos would go on to win this title three more times with other partners. Stoklos was also named as the AVP's MVP three times during his career (1988, 1989, and 1991). Off the court, Stoklos appeared in a number of advertisements and in the 1990 film *Side Out!*. In 2008, he was inducted into the Volleyball Hall of Fame.

STEVE TIMMONS

One player who doesn't know how to leave an Olympics without a medal is Steve Timmons. He represented the United States on the men's indoor volleyball team three times and received a bronze and two gold medals. He played in the outside hitter position and is best known for his powerful attacks. He is also one of the first players to hit from the back row. Timmons was born on November 29, 1958, in Newport Beach, California. The young Timmons played volleyball at Newport Harbor High School and then at Orange Coast College and the University of Southern California. He joined the U.S. team in 1983. At the 1984 Olympics, he helped the team beat Brazil and get a gold medal. Timmons was also named MVP for his efforts. In the 1988 Games, the team also took home the gold, and in 1992, it won a bronze. Timmons was also an excellent beach volleyball player and spent 1987–1994 touring with the premiere beach volleyball league, AVP, and collecting over $100,000 in winnings. Now retired from competitive play, Timmons owned a sportswear company called Redsand that he sold in 2004.

LOGAN TOM

The woman who has the honor of being the youngest woman chosen to play on the U.S. Olympic volleyball team is Logan Maile Lei Tom. She qualified for the 2000 Olympic Games in Sydney when she was just 19. Tom was born on May 25, 1981, in Napa, California. She plays both indoor and beach volleyball in the position of outside hitter. As of 2014, she is a four-time Olympian, having played with the U.S. indoor volleyball team in 2000, 2004, 2008, and 2012. In each of the last two Olympics, the U.S. team won the silver medal, and in the 2008 Games, Tom was named best scorer. From 2004–2007, Tom took a break from indoor volleyball and focused on beach volleyball. She returned to indoor volleyball in 2007 and was named one of the three most valuable players at the FIVB World Cup. She continues to collect accolades for her skills, including being named best receiver at the 2010 World Championships and best server (in addition to winning a gold medal) at the 2011 NORCECA Championship. In 2013, she was inducted into the Stanford University Hall of Fame.

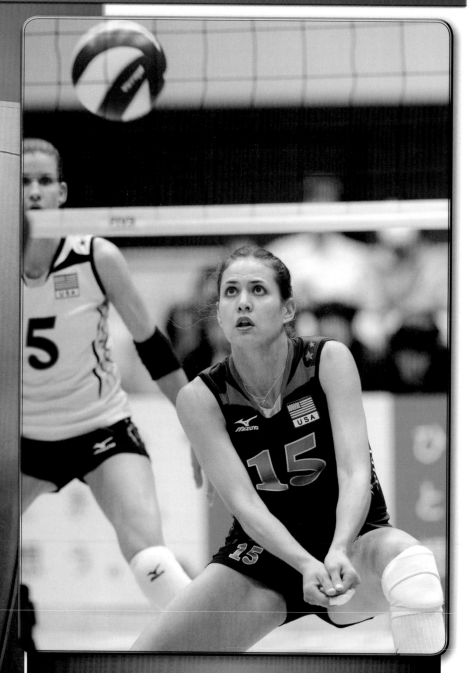

Logan Tom eyes the ball as it approaches during a preliminary match of the 2010 FIVB World Championships. Toshifumi Kitamura/AFP/Getty Images

RON VON HAGEN

Often called the "Babe Ruth of beach volleyball," Ron Von Hagen is a legend in the sport. In many ways, he has set the benchmark against which all players are measured. Von Hagen was born on November 23, 1938. As a young man, he excelled at many sports and didn't actually take an interest in volleyball until his senior year at the University of California, Los Angeles (UCLA). However, once he found volleyball, he never looked back. From 1962 until 1978, Von Hagen played in 120 tournaments, winning more than half (62) of them. As a defense specialist, he was known for his focus and ability to handle particularly difficult passes and digs. He was also known for his intense training and strengthening regimen, which he followed year-round—testament to his incredible drive to win. Von Hagen had several strong partnerships throughout his career, but none was more successful than the historic partnership he formed with Ron Lang in 1966. Combining Von Hagen's defensive skills with Lang's command of game mechanics and excellence at hitting and setting, the duo earned 28 Open titles together, 15 of which they captured in just two years (1966–68). Von Hagen went

63

on to give more stellar performances, setting numerous records. He won 60 of 100 consecutive Open tournaments, placing second or third in 30 of the other 40 tournaments. For another record, he placed in the top three at 54 consecutive tournaments. Although many of his records were eventually broken, Von Hagen remains a model for players today. Despite his incredible success rate, Von Hagen was never in it for the money. In fact, his career earnings amounted to a total of $625. He was inducted into the Beach Volleyball Hall of Fame and the Volleyball Hall of Fame in 1992.

KERRI WALSH JENNINGS

American Kerri Walsh established herself as one of the top beach volleyball players in the world in the early 21st century. With her partner, Misty May-Treanor, she won Olympic gold medals in the event in 2004, 2008, and 2012.

Walsh was born on August 15, 1978, in Santa Clara, California.

She attended Stanford University, where she played indoor volleyball and helped her team win consecutive National Collegiate Athletic Association indoor volleyball titles in 1996 and 1997; she was named national coplayer of the year in 1999. She moved on to play for the U.S. indoor volleyball team at the 2000

Kerri Walsh (left) *watches her partner, Misty May-Treanor, during a match at the 2005 FIVB Beach Volleyball World Championships.* **Alexander Hassenstein/Bongarts/Getty Images**

Olympic Games in Sydney, Australia, which finished fourth overall.

In 2001, Walsh teamed up on the sand with May, and the next year they reached the world number-one ranking. In 2003, they won a then-record 90 straight matches and all eight tournaments in which they played, including the world championships, where they upset the defending Brazilian champions in the final. At the 2004 Olympics in Athens, Greece, they became the first American female duo to win gold medals in beach volleyball. They followed up their success in Athens by capturing two more world titles, in 2005 and 2007. Meanwhile, Walsh married volleyball player Casey Jennings in December 2005.

In 2008 Walsh and May-Treanor (Misty May had married professional baseball player Matt Treanor in 2004) competed at the Olympic Games in Beijing, China, and they became the first beach volleyball team to win consecutive Olympic gold medals. The final match, in which they defeated Wang Jie and Tian Jia of China 21–18, 21–18, marked the pair's 108th consecutive victory and their 14th straight Olympics win (they did not lose a set either in Beijing or in Athens at the 2004 Olympics). They extended their consecutive victory streak to 112 before losing at the end of August 2008. Walsh later took time off from competing to start a family and gave birth to two sons, one in 2009 and the second in 2010. She and May-Treanor returned as a team to international competition in 2011 and claimed the silver medal at the world championships that year.

At the 2012 Olympic Games in London, England, Walsh and May-Treanor won their third straight Olympic gold medal, defeating fellow Americans April Ross and Jennifer Kessy 21–16, 21–16 in the final. Walsh and May-Treanor went unbeaten in London (dropping only one set during the preliminary round), and with their final victory, they extended their Olympic winning streak to 21 straight matches. Walsh partnered with Ross in 2013, following May-Treanor's retirement in 2012.

PAULA WEISHOFF

Paula Weishoff is a member of the Volleyball Hall of Fame, competed in the Olympics three times, and collected a number of medals in international competition throughout her career. Weishoff was born May 1, 1962, in Hollywood, California. She began playing volleyball in middle school, and by high school had established herself as a talented player, lettering in volleyball as well as in track, soccer, and

Paula Weishoff answers questions during a press conference at the University of California, Irvine, where she has been head women's volleyball coach since 2009. © **The Orange County Register/ ZUMA Press**

softball. While still in high school, Weishoff traveled to Colorado to attend a sports festival and compete against other young female volleyball players from the United States. She also tried out for and earned a chance to play in her first international competition: the Pacific Rim Tournament in Hawaii. From there, she continued to play volleyball and excel, earning accolades at amateur events, including a silver medal at the 1979 U.S. Olympic Festival and the MVP title at the 1980 U.S. Junior Olympics.

Weishoff enrolled at the University of Southern California (USC) for college but left in 1981 to join the U.S. national team. The team gained medals at a number of international competitions, including a silver medal at the 1984 Olympic Games. Weishoff was named the MVP of the team. In 1984, she moved to Italy and joined the Italian League, with whom she played for nine seasons. She would return to the United States and again play with the U.S. women's team in the Olympics in 1992. While the U.S. team took bronze, Weishoff was named MVP of the entire women's Olympic volleyball competition. She participated in the 1996 Olympics and retired from competitive volleyball in 1997. Weishoff was inducted into the Volleyball Hall of Fame in 1998. She returned to college at USC and earned a B.A. degree in 2000. She also assumed coaching duties, first as assistant coach of the women's volleyball team at USC (1997–2003) and later as head coach of the women's volleyball team, initially at Concordia University Irvine (2004–09) and, since 2009, at the University of California, Irvine.

These men and women are just a few of those who have contributed to the sport of volleyball. As of 2014, there are 112 men and women hailing from 21 different countries who have all been inducted into the Volleyball Hall of Fame. The sport of volleyball requires extreme focus, timing, speed, strength, and above all, communication and teamwork. It takes great dedication to master all of the skills, from executing a perfect pass or digging a ball inches from the floor to delivering an unstoppable spike. From novices to masters, the sport is as fun to play as it is to watch. As volleyball continues to grow and gain popularity, it will be exciting to see what new players will bring to the sport.

accolade An award or an expression of praise.

agility The ability to move quickly and easily.

block A defensive move that stops a ball from coming over the net and either sends the ball back over the net or slows the ball for a teammate to return.

circumference The length of a line that goes around something.

conditioning Training to improve at a certain activity.

dig A defensive shot in which the forearms are used, often when receiving a hard-driven ball.

environs The surroundings or the vicinity of an area.

juggernaut An unstoppable force.

libero A special player who acts as the team's defensive specialist.

match A contest (as in volleyball) completed when one player or side wins a specified number of sets or games.

officiating Acting as an official in a sporting event.

Open A competition (such as a volleyball tournament) that allows both professionals and amateurs to participate.

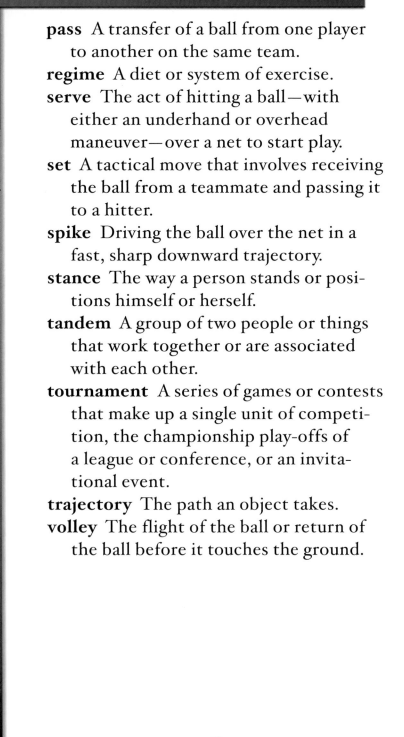

pass A transfer of a ball from one player to another on the same team.

regime A diet or system of exercise.

serve The act of hitting a ball—with either an underhand or overhead maneuver—over a net to start play.

set A tactical move that involves receiving the ball from a teammate and passing it to a hitter.

spike Driving the ball over the net in a fast, sharp downward trajectory.

stance The way a person stands or positions himself or herself.

tandem A group of two people or things that work together or are associated with each other.

tournament A series of games or contests that make up a single unit of competition, the championship play-offs of a league or conference, or an invitational event.

trajectory The path an object takes.

volley The flight of the ball or return of the ball before it touches the ground.

Fédération Internationale de Volleyball (FIVB)
Ch. Edouard-Sandoz 2-4
1006 Lausanne
Switzerland
Website: http://www.fivb.org
The FIVB is the governing body responsible for organizing competitions for all forms of volleyball globally. Each year the organization puts on events showcasing the best in men's and women's volleyball, both indoor and beach.

Ontario Volleyball Association (OVA)
3 Concorde Gate, Suite 304
Toronto, ON M3C 3N7
Canada
(416) 426-7316
Website: http://www.ontariovolleyball.org
The OVA is dedicated to helping Ontarians discover and enjoy the sport of volleyball at all levels of play. The organization runs programs in indoor volleyball, beach volleyball, and even volleyball from a seated position.

USA Volleyball (USAV)
4065 Sinton Road, Suite 200
Colorado Springs, CO 80907
(719) 228-6800

Website: http://www.teamusa.org

USA Volleyball is the national governing body for the sport of volleyball in the United States. Its goal is to provide growth, enhancement, and competitive success for volleyball players within the United States.

Volleyball Canada

1084 Kenaston Street, Unit 1A

Ottowa, ON K1B 3P5

Canada

(613) 748-5681

Website: http://www.volleyball.ca

This organization, which joined the FIVB in 1953, is devoted to fostering the growth and development of the sport of volleyball in Canada.

Volleyball Hall of Fame

444 Dwight Street

Holyoke, MA 01040

(413) 536-0926

Website: http://www.volleyhall.org

The Volleyball Hall of Fame honors the extraordinary players, coaches, officials, and other leaders in the sport of volleyball. The museum contains treasured artifacts of the sport and those who have contributed to it. It is located in Holyoke, Massachusetts, the birthplace of volleyball.

Volleyball Magazine
Madavor Media LLC
25 Braintree Hill Office Park, Suite 404
Braintree, MA 02184
(617) 706-9110
Website: http://www.volleyballmag.com
This magazine provides information on all
aspects of the game of volleyball, including
coverage of competitions and events, nutri-
tion and fitness tutorials, game tips, and
conversations with the sport's top leaders.

WEBSITES

Because of the changing nature of Internet links, Rosen Publishing has developed an online list of websites related to the subject of this book. This site is updated regularly. Please use this link to access this list:

http://www.rosenlinks.com/SPOR/Voll

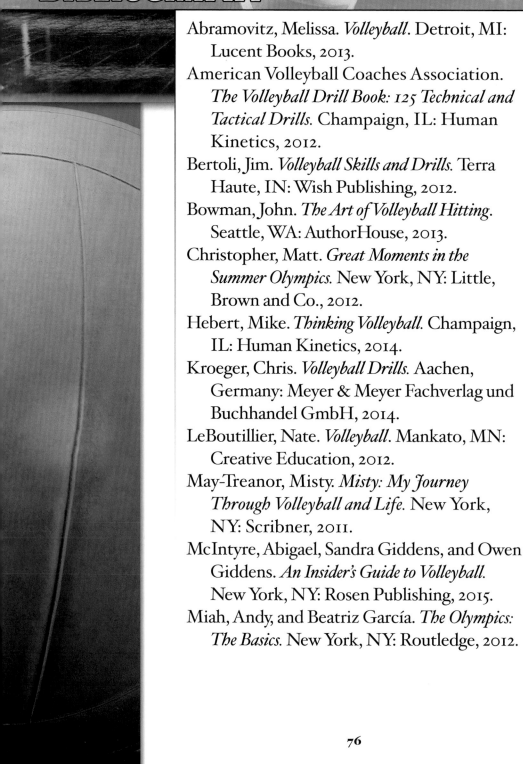

Abramovitz, Melissa. *Volleyball*. Detroit, MI: Lucent Books, 2013.

American Volleyball Coaches Association. *The Volleyball Drill Book: 125 Technical and Tactical Drills*. Champaign, IL: Human Kinetics, 2012.

Bertoli, Jim. *Volleyball Skills and Drills*. Terra Haute, IN: Wish Publishing, 2012.

Bowman, John. *The Art of Volleyball Hitting*. Seattle, WA: AuthorHouse, 2013.

Christopher, Matt. *Great Moments in the Summer Olympics*. New York, NY: Little, Brown and Co., 2012.

Hebert, Mike. *Thinking Volleyball*. Champaign, IL: Human Kinetics, 2014.

Kroeger, Chris. *Volleyball Drills*. Aachen, Germany: Meyer & Meyer Fachverlag und Buchhandel GmbH, 2014.

LeBoutillier, Nate. *Volleyball*. Mankato, MN: Creative Education, 2012.

May-Treanor, Misty. *Misty: My Journey Through Volleyball and Life*. New York, NY: Scribner, 2011.

McIntyre, Abigael, Sandra Giddens, and Owen Giddens. *An Insider's Guide to Volleyball*. New York, NY: Rosen Publishing, 2015.

Miah, Andy, and Beatriz García. *The Olympics: The Basics*. New York, NY: Routledge, 2012.

Miller, Bob. *The Volleyball Handbook.*
Champaign, IL: Human Kinetics, 2013.

Oldenburg, Steve. *Complete Conditioning for Volleyball.* Champaign, IL: Human Kinetics, 2015.

Spooner, Edward. *The Science of Volleyball: Practice Development and Drill Design.* Bloomington, IN: iUniverse, 2012.

USA Volleyball. *Volleyball: Systems & Strategies.* Champaign, IL: Human Kinetics, 2009.

Waite, Pete. *Aggressive Volleyball.* Champaign, IL: Human Kinetics, 2009.

Yasuda, Anita. *Beach Volleyball Is No Joke.* Mankato, MN: Sports Illustrated Kids, 2011.